# MAHREM

# Edward Foster

# MAHREM
# Things Men Should
# Do for Men

## A Suite for O

"He who is unable to live in society, or who has no need because
he is sufficient for himself, must be either a beast or a god."
—Aristotle, *Politics*, trans. Benjamin Jowett

"Between ourselves, I have ever observed supercelestial opinions
and subterranean manners to be of singular accord."
—Montaigne, "Of Experience," trans. Charles Cotton

Marsh Hawk Press
New York City

·(⇄)·

These poems are for Toprak, with gratitude

·(⇄)·

Library of Congress Cataloging-in-Publication Data

Foster, Edward Halsey.
  Mahrem : things men should do for men : a suite for O / Edward
Foster.
     p. cm.
  ISBN 0-9713332-5-4
  1. Middle East—Poetry. I. Title.
  PS3556.O7592 M34 2002
  811'.54—dc21

                                          2002005911

·(⇄)·

Text: Bell
Titles: Caslon

·(⇄)·

The author is grateful to Joseph Donahue, editor of the special section
of *Titanic Operas* (2002) in which the following poems were first published:
"My Most Dishonest Feature Is My Name," "Sophisticates of Language Live
Alone," "Statius Among the Shades," "I Wind My Fingers Round Your Wrist,"
"Love," "This Time Your Liquid Skin Will Suck," "The Night Bright Tellak
Came a God," and "Your Paper Core of Anger Now Can Burn."

# CONTENTS

# BY WAY OF PREFACE

"Things are what they are experienced as." —John Dewey

The photographs in this book are not directly related to individual poems but may suggest a particular world or sovereignty which cannot be reduced to language yet in which these poems were first possible.

The photographs suggest this sovereignty as seen and valued by one who in Turkish would be called an "ecnebi" — an outsider, a stranger, a foreigner.

Politically the site is modern Turkey, but that region inherits much that is traceable to the beginnings of history and, absorbed into various and distinct cultures, now appears so instinctive and unaffected as to be all but beyond naming.

It is this endowment (as one might call it) and not the country that the poems concern.

Some may feel that the poems imply "Orientalism," the appropriation of another culture as exotic, quaint, and strange.

This is not, however, the intention nor is it the experience.

It is, rather, an experience that allows recognitions that elsewhere might not occur or that in the West are now conventionally framed as if they were political and are thus made both common and obscure.

# ECNEBİ

*for Toprak*

"The world of any moment is the merest appearance."
—Ralph Waldo Emerson, "The American Scholar"

In walkways and *pasaje*s
Shoeshine boys will say,
   they always say,
Mister, have you wife?
You want girl?
I bring you girl.

You want boy? I think
I bring you boy.

But someone's
   always watching, my dear friend.
You cannot bring me boy.

Mister, you like boy.
I bring you boy.

# NO DECISION ON MY LOOK ALIKE

Line them up and all boys look the same.
Each country has its faces.
Those should count
                    but no. — We
learn from poets whom we don't remember now
that language hardly matters:
they act as if those memories
were set aside.

Show the men along
the beach. Attract me so.
The photos fade. Watch how boys
— inch by inch — can disappear.
And reappear.

# THE SORDID MAN

has changed rigidities for cash.
He even keeps a register for tips.
He wants more now for friends and lives
a rumpled life, his tunic riding up his knees
as he runs by. He is the coarsest Roman,
the man who calculates the cost of sacrament.
With him such things are flint — contention,
mental blaze.

Dear youth, he thinks you are the rain
that clarifies his sky.

# THE BRUISE THAT COULD IMPROVE US ALL

*for Jon*

Mendicants take barges on the Thames.
Young boys listen, too far beyond the ladies
to annoy. The old man sitting
bends to watch. His hands sway gently
down between his thighs. He knows the lesson
that the ladies teach and does not care.
The young boys hear,
too far beyond the ladies to annoy.

# THE MAN IN THE BOX

He had his payoff when the boy believed his lover,
called around (you call me, I call you),
and old men acted decent, signaling
to ladies much too old to look.
So do you want to be a learned man?

The couples separate into
their separate rooms.
The payoffs all are good,
though that part doesn't matter,
doesn't chill,
does not invite sufficient wrath.

# BEYOĞLU

*for Volkan*

Never did the finer toys they want to be
dance so well as in your hand that links us in my
mind. All those stupid couples in the street
fall out of need sooner that your hand
can drop away. They leave their street
whose chilly wind blew through my race to meet,
but you could be my poet even if I never need
to know your name,
gentle chill, who would meet me
only when you're kind.
I ask to wake with you.

# ALL FRIENDSHIPS END THE SAME

*for Tuncay*

You're still sweet, Mr. Wall,
but sweet is not enough. Your
trieds-and-true are buried
in your flame. The tall boy cooks
but lithely cooks: he's not in love with you.
Compatriots are central to my life —
you once were mine.

# YILDIRIM BUILDS HIS TOWER

Dear friend. Bring him close, my sword.
All day we can rescind, reject. And purify
our Arabic demand. When so, he's here.
Give wives and history due. And tell him who
you are. The boy is gracious,
and what's most, my dear —
he looks at us,
fears neither me nor you.

# MY MOST DISHONEST FEATURE IS MY NAME

Flowered silk beyond his schooling.
What's left to leave except you bring him home?
We're not told who's been teaching whom.
Elder statesmen classify his kind.

The pious poet writes us out of life.
It's Easter: resurrection's easy if you trust.
Lie back and comb your hand through hair.
My hair.

     The sea is resurrected
with the wind. The flowered silk reflects
my likeness now.

     Resurrection,
statesmen, pious poets,
leave or touch his hand as silk.
Never tell me who is kind.

# MY AMBER LIGHT GOES OFF

This was the end of caring —
We'd no longer drink so to forget.
The terminus was fine. We'd know that
single living has its busy law,
interrupting when we most would care.

Confession's not enough.
Why do they make of it a god?
But time and tide. Admission resonates
today with someone fair.

# THE BLESSED WALL COMES DOWN

                        I met
the young boy once to contradict his stare:
the taste of salt rolled swiftly on my tongue.
I contradict the stare.
                    The garden out
beneath my room is walled. I'd never make
a garden there.
                    Gentlemen do that.
                            I
contradict their cause.

He cleans his face and
still would be alone. In movement, I am
half-aware. These children will be men.
I hope to feel their joy again.

# YOU STAND BESIDE THE ROAD
# IN AUTOMATIC PRIDE

*for Adam*

Each new complexity is based on hope.
Why, Master Due, has memory a part
in every sound? What music's eating you?
Adam's habit's not so good, perhaps,
for me. With you, what counts is clocks
and automatic sound.

Revise, revise: must all work
have its bitter end?

Stir self, dear master,
Adam. Please don't sit so near.

# SOPHISTICATES OF LANGUAGE LIVE ALONE

The palace doors are shut. Gide
wanders healthy on the street. Generous and
limited in need, he says no palace
yet contains his creed.

I'd lengthen your reserve,
you say. I'd teach submission.
The doors won't open here again.
Remission, children, help me, please.

# STATIUS AMONG THE SHADES

Last night the food was set.
All things were washed.
The room, I thought, had lost
its age. I waited,
then went for a walk.
No poems, poets met me there.

Today we keep it simple.
He's at work. I watch the children
in the park below. All color
every morning still is amber, red.

# MUSEUMS MADE OF

Well, an evening in the park.
Impatient there,
you can't be real. Walk by.

Our sounds are low; neighbors
can't be here. True: try again.
Our patience still can bear to wait.
Museums are for merry men,
and I remember this as well,
your cagey wildness in the dark.

# NECESSARY GRIEF

"We animate what we can,
and see only what we animate."
—Ralph Waldo Emerson, "Experience"


No promise, none to alter.
Anatolia's black with sun.
Oh, O, please let me in
this time to go around
the room like Greeks,
whoever does it, thinking as
you said we'd think.

# AS WE SPEAK, ENEMIES WITHDRAW

"as a root out of a dry ground" —Isaiah, 53:2


No pardons, please. These monsters had
no lesser field in which to meet. The parents
in our dream set out to seek a light. Your
arms are tempting as you sleep.
None's here, so let me touch your shoulder
with my hand.

The visionary poet said we all have second sight.
The picture helps, but I remember, too,
when I felt as you feel and so could pass
an arm along your neck and down your back.
Outside the parents plead. The images
release, and as we reach around new solid form,
they seize, and shower down,
as we complete whatever dissipates our sleep.

# SORRY TO DISTURB YOU

And we're then thankful for that little lip of skin —
So, thinking how my audience at home,
whoever they may be, would relish that
fine moment, as to say, "Oh, look again,
my padre, papa, pippa passes, you're
the loadstone we adore."

                                 Give me lips,
live skin, no labias of love, but longing,
listless, while I lie with you upon the floor
and suck your little lip and make it sore.

# ONE MONTH

Resolve the month with careless fear.
Dissipate control. Watch clothing, clocks,
the things you bought, be auctioned to the old.
This day we say there's nothing left to know.

And now you're watched, not watching.

The elderly, no longer friends,
congregate and sit. They watch,
infringe your sight with weary pomp.

You gather up whatever's left.
No one now to speak, be spoken to.
You find the door,
look back to know they're there,
for then or them to go.

# THREE-FINGERED INTELLECT

Meeting you, I thought this "second best"
is not so bad. I'd still fuck you,
and, given your emotion and restraint,
what more could any ask? You're younger,
somewhat more reluctant to despair.
Should I need more? What kind of man
rolls over saying (in effect), "Don't wait on me
to wait on you."
                 Oh, never could there be
a wanting: satisfaction means to please.
Your memories of Rome and someone younger
held me in your thrall. It truly was your self
I wanted, made somewhat small.

# PETER AND PAUL

We're painting all our walls a deeper hue.
We hope it's dark enough to keep you out.
Sorry, Paul.

As all now know, you could be
generous at night.

And you were kind.
But we like passion, Peter,
not your yellow
regiments,
locks,
reason,
light.

## HE WANTED A PERSONAL LIFE

Lime kilns melt the marble, what would
be marble. Hardness in your hands
was sin. Error's error lay in satisfaction,
Ethan. Go ahead. Pick it up again.

We want to hold things still, hence your
hand against my thigh. "This will bore."
But no. The only thing that bores me now is
what we didn't do today. The only thing I want
is finding this time how.

# SALT

Grazed skin, passable, then more,
and as in Raphael,
a face too fair for fairness to resist.
Sweet taste of Asia,
London on the edge,
Paris, Rome, New York.
The tongue held sweetly,
light between my lips.

Said one man then:
take women, take my wife.
Ah, no, sad me,
— sad you:
keep that one to yourself.
I'd rather take the ocean,
drinking all I can,
and swill the salt to wash
away her taste,
and skin.

# I WIND MY FINGERS ROUND YOUR WRIST

The poppies on the Asian shore begin to bloom,
but my heart's bitter. I'm not allowed to say
which things I'd wish. Who's young beside this
Turkish shore? Who'd say it more?
Why can't I say wherever I would be?

Skip money (he had said); I want to be with you.
— Well, change your verse to issues: happenstance
and cognitive concerns. But tell me true,
                              my loving one:
who's leaving me to be with you?

# BREAKING THE STREAM

Lady, you'd once make my pleasure to invest.
My clothes could be your mockery today,
but I'll not dress for you again,
or you for me. You look quite reasoned now.
Growing old, you're mainly
growing old. Your large frame,
title, house are deeply sad.
You're now the sick delight songs
never need. Futures imitate your worst
regard. Lady, you were once my
Persian garden. You were sweet
to taste. The children in the courtyard
whispered you. I cannot hear them now.
Nor can they you.

# DREYER

Until he'd wish to know —
as you spoon feed the dying man.
Always children seem a little older than they are,
knowing what they cannot know again.
They have their comfort: keep their
house alone and light the lamp.

The books are sure. Perhaps they are
the only things until you touch or I touch you.
We watch the older friends and know their care.

I shouldn't care with patterns woven
in the air.

Feed the dying man, who will not sleep,
and says he'll care,
so I draw near and kiss
him on his hair.

# BEYOĞLU (2)

In this, the words run cold —
your face becomes a cutout
in the light. Shout it down, and
yes, I care: the face is just
an oval line. You were me once.
Now only I can take that image home,
a cutout for my book.
                    In saying this,
I know the words are cold without
a wish for greener change.
Now pearls can frighten you.
The words run cold as all
the merchants shut up shop.
The boys are costly now.
Your face was once as lively
as the gardens in the park.
The light slants down.
I can no longer take your face
and bring it down to satisfy
my lead. Though when the door
is shut, I merely say you're much too
cloistered in your need.

# WIND IN THE WILLOWS

Toad grasps his pole.
We watch him closer than we watch ourselves.
We have the time to take on things like this.
Flagrant, part of this our world, and most of it
extinct. Memory's now what counts, my friend
would say, and tells me he has reasons not to care.
So do we all, but once we wanted these,
and seeing him, we know we want them still.
The young on side streets see us true
but never see as much as we see them.
Gentle Toad, let's build a fire with your hall.

# QUEEN-SIZED MATTRESS FOR THE DEAD

This is a question for your class,
   which I haven't been attending,
   M.
But what am I to say if you
   remove yourself, like sleet,
from every thought I make?
   My clowning only makes you
closer, brighter. There's no one
   left tonight to fake.

Go back to your computer,
   gentle M.,
and type.

Submission's not a measure
(though yes it is):
type, type, type.

# LOVE

Take your prick in hand
and move it slowly.
Take his and
bring it to your mouth.
Feel just what you've
been told: to feel.
Imagine this: the grand boy
beating back your prick.
Move into him.

# THE LAND OF THE CAT

Dream of vacant doorways,
man now, no boy, no passing in.
A language made with shadows of
a god — precede the eye.
The doorway's vacant — no man,
no boy to pass. Respect means
no one comes, at least to you.
The passage can turn dark with holy eyes,
a passage full of eyes.
The men, the boys are gone.
Only eyes that can't see now remain,
my shadows of a god.

# THIS TIME YOUR LIQUID SKIN WILL SUCK

This time your liquid skin will suck.
(My turn to wait.) The streets are night with boys
as joy. The quest this evening's
full of talk. I only wish the other one
were you, running after me —
and not this I, as always,
running after you.

# DE RERUM NATURA

"Già il veleno l'ha rosa!"
—Scarpia in Puccini, *Tosca*


In allegory I can fashion hands
that know the things they need.
Break down the background, leaving
persons in the view. I studied you,
these years, to quote you as I'd guide
myself. Each time I'd see
without your sense you'd need
me here or ask I'd move toward you.
No, friend, I'm not the thing we see,
nor you, though this possess me now
and fashion hands an ecstacy.

# MEN WHO THREATEN MEN

We sell our books, give cash
for education, try to make our
lives reverberate again.

You've heard the names and narrative before.
This version isn't ours, but anyone will do
to hurt a friend. We give our lives to work —
just so we then can watch our bodies
sway before the mirror,
sterling in the night:
there are no pleasures equal in the street.
Images can satisfy the need,
projecting profiles made of greed.

# THE NIGHT BRIGHT TELLAK CAME A GOD

*for Halis*

A sweater would do him good.
Rose, lavender, spice, dark-skinned
Kurdish sweat. Our light's indifferent
to logical display. I'd rather
take my strength in friends. How men
can be like this, I've never known.
He, I (and you?) can do it, though.
Dear Levantine: this Kurd is made
from images, a surrogate for me —
swell tight, bright anger in my bed.

# THERE ARE NO ACCIDENTS

*for Murad*

Disease is final. Only your dark
skin can save me now. Your hair is
taut. Your mind dissects my luxury.
We give it all we've got,
but your profession here beneath the
cellars of my care is fraught with
phlegm, blood, sperm of young men,
dead. I trusted you. You gave no choice.
You might deceive yourself, and yet
I thought it could be fine, this once,
to measure up, a Greek in you.

47

# LANGUAGE MEANS TO TAKE

"What is useful for one is not useful for another."
—Théophile Gautier, *Mademoiselle de Maupin*


You wait. Submission means a gift is never
yours until you let it go. You can't expect
or bank on some new flaw. Approach is all.
No sooner do you get a moment of delight than
lights go up: wisdom's in the other man.
I practice piety but only try it on.
The flower's always black. Dear you,
this last time: please.

# YOUR PAPER CORE OF ANGER NOW CAN BURN

Sheep, *raya*, on the upland plane.
They graze, almost spring. Night never comes.
Anticipation's not enough. Your hope
is your command:
    hope's not enough.
The sheep will graze, the shepherd
has his hard-won grace. Night never comes.
The watchdog sees the flock. Lie still.
You now are home. He is not.

# THE PURITAN FROM BLACHERNAE

*for Joe Donahue*

*Mehmet the Conqueror wished for his pleasure the son of the Grand Duke. The young man was lovely, his skin almost olive. But the Grand Duke believed the Sultan would corrupt his son and said no. So the Grand Duke watched the Sultan's soldiers kill his son, and then the soldiers made the Grand Duke kneel before the Sultan and kiss his boots as he in turn was killed.*

Iron chairs on the portico,
the pillars stacked in the garden.
In Istanbul there's everything:
the dissenter dies kissing the boots
of the man he'd betray.

The Minotaur's lost in the palace;
the draperies hold odors of spice.
Bellini sketches the Sultan,
his peacocks walk in the rain.

The thunderclouds thicken,
but no one knows not to remain.
The tulips on columns promise
us joy. Up Turkish steps, the
young men grow richer in trade.

# PHOTOGRAPHS

*The photograph on p. 13 was taken in Izmir, the photograph on p. 27 in Ankara, and the rest in Istanbul.*

p. 13: ceremonial circumcision clothes

p. 20: apartment building, Beyoğlu (formerly Pera, the old European district of Istanbul)

pp. 24: boy selling gum on Istiklal Cadessi, formerly the Grande Rue de Pera

p. 27: a section of the oldest part of Ankara, settled in the Bronze Age and occupied successively by Hittites, Persians, Romans, Byzantines, Ottomans, and many other peoples

p. 33: Rüstem Pasha Mosque

p. 40: boys in their circumcision clothes

p. 45: köşk, Topkapı Sarayı

# NOTES

*Mahrem*: Turkish/Arabic term for "beloved" but with emphasis on "the you that I am."

pp. vii and 1: *ecnebi* (edge-ne-bee): stranger, outsider, foreigner, especially one from the West (Turkish).

p. 1: *pasaj*: arcade (Turkish).

pp. 7, 35: *Beyoğlu*: the Turkish name for what was formerly called Pera, a section of Istanbul long known for pleasure and intrigue.

p. 10: *Yildirim* ("Thunderbolt"): Sultan Yildirim Bayezit (1389-1402) built the castle known as Anadoluhisari on the Asian side of the Bosphorus in 1393 as part of his campaign (ultimately unsuccessful) to capture Constantinople.

p. 17: *Statius*: In canto 21 of Dante's *Purgatorio*, Statius wishes to honor Virgil, but Virgil reminds him (in Allen Mandlebaum's translation): "Brother, there's no need / you are a shade, a shade is what you see."

p. 28: *Ethan*: Ethan Brand in Hawthorne's story of that name.

p. 44: *tellak*: a *masseur* (Turkish); during the Ottoman era, the *tellak* was often a young man or boy who was also a prostitute.

p. 49: *raya*: protected peoples under Ottoman rule (literally "sheep").